From
Darkening
Porches

From Darkening Porches

POEMS BY
Jo McDougall

THE UNIVERSITY OF
ARKANSAS PRESS
FAYETTEVILLE   1996

Designed by Gail Carter

⊖ The paper used in this publication meets the minimum
requirements of the American National Standard for Perma-
nence of Paper for Printed Library Materials Z39.48-1984.

Library of Congress Cataloging-in-Publication Data

McDougall, Jo.
      From darkening porches : poems / by Jo McDougall.
          p. cm.
      ISBN 1-55728-407-5 (cloth : alk. paper). —
      ISBN 1-55728-408-3 (pbk. alk. paper)
      I. Title.
      PS3563.C3586F76   1996
      811'.54—dc20   95-36191
                                          CIP

For

Tanner, Lauren, Shea, Chandler, Collin, and Merritt
&
in memory of my father

Acknowledgments

Thanks to the editors of the following publications where these poems, some with different titles and in slightly different versions, first appeared: *The Quarterly, Midwest Quarterly, Slow Dancer, Controlled Burn, Ohio State University Journal, Kansas Voices, Louisiana Literature, The Rio Grande Review, Women Who Marry Houses* from Coyote Love Press, and from *Roots and Recognition: Where Does Poetry Come From?* published by The Friends of Timmons Chapel, Pittsburg State University.

Special thanks to Pittsburg State University and to The MacDowell Colony for a sabbatical and a fellowship, respectively, affording me time for this book to come to be.

CONTENTS

What Happens When We Leave

Leaving a room, we remember arriving,
the first turning of the key,
the room, pristine and startled,
opening to take us in.
Dropping the key on the bureau,
we open a door

someplace else.

Behind us now, the room goes mute.
The morning paper sifts to the floor,
ticking itself to sleep.
The desk and chair and table,
nothing expected of them,
settle their hands behind them
like morticians at the church.

The sound of a crow.
Then the electric sweeper. The witch inside it
boiling the carpet.

Late afternoon.
A simmer of traffic. A far train.

Then dusk.
Silence deepens in the room,
seamless as an apple
or a fox.

Then footsteps.
Outside the door the brushing of a sleeve,
someone else with the expectant key,
absently humming.

NIGHTS AND DAYS

Nights, the dream.
I'm on a dirt road
trying to outrun Kansas:
the blisters in the farmhouse paint,
the ripples in the wheat
like horsehide under flies.
Days, the wind rounding the corners of the house
like a warp of bees.

SHE REFLECTS UPON A SADNESS

She will not say
that it was ennobling, that there must have been
a purpose.

She will say
that if it had not happened
she might not feel this rush of joy
like a blush
at the sight of a hawk dropping into a ditch,
ignoring the traffic, taking
what it needs.

CIRCUS

The elephants entered town
from some country the other side of God.
As solemn and as bored as saints,
they seemed to step to music
we couldn't hear.
Then men with tents and costumes
and ropes as big as trees
swarmed the lot across from the drive-in.

When the young trapezist
swam the air to his death
that hazy afternoon,
I didn't see it.
I was watching the elephants turn in the ring
like toys winding down.
I was watching dust
turn in the light like sequins.

Then, always on a night we weren't thinking of it,
the circus would leave.
I was glad to see it go
although it has taken me
nearly a lifetime
to admit it.

A Bottomlands Farmer Deals with the Arkansas Power and Light Transmission Towers Set in His Field

for Jim Spicer

He resents what they take:
his best field, the one that drained right,
a road his grandfather built.
Since they set the towers
his cows don't calve.
The bald spot in the winter wheat
could hold six tractors abreast.
Maybe he'll sell the place.
But who'd want it now?

The farmer sees his father under a full moon,
riding the bucking Farmall, plowing straight.
"Always somebody out there," he used to say,
"biding his time."

RADIO

The house on Mickle Road.
Ten o'clock evenings,
my father turning off his Philco,
the orange light reluctant to go.
And didn't the brocade where the sound came out
get hot, and smell?
I think it did, a faint scorching,
the brocade a shade of brown
you don't find anymore.

EIGHT YEARS A GHOST

He thinks I keep his things.
He thinks I hear him whistling.
He thinks he's making a racket
on the stairs.

THE TIME OF THEIR LIVES

At the cinema
they find their lives.
The years stop nattering.
There's music
as they take off their clothes, or kiss.
Their bodies glimmer
like dolphins in moonlight.
The lights go up.
On the black floor the dirty popcorn.
The man and the woman
suddenly pale and blinking.

THE CRIB AT BUFFALO ANTIQUES

I touch the crib,
seeing the mother and the father and the preacher,
the wind on a hill,
the shovels nicking the small stones.

SPINSTERS

In that house
a radio was keeping its dull distance.
A clock struck in the metallic way a rooster announces day.
One of the women was in a bedroom,
sewing on a treadle machine
in fits and starts
as if listening for something.
A burglar perhaps, or the dog recruiting a shoe
for the porch.
Neither happened.
A breeze stirred up dust from the stockyards next door
and a cousin called
from Minneapolis.

THE DUPLEX

It's a little run down, but okay. I hope
we can afford it, with layoffs at the plant,
one baby sick, another on the way.
The neighborhood is iffy, but it beats the trailer.

Dwayne, my husband, put up the swing set
over there next to that little maple.
I wish this place had another tree.
The babies, they'll come to use it later, of course;
for now, the swing set is for Jimmy. He's five
this October, going to pre-school.
We got it cheap. It looks real good though,
all red and green and shining, the slide so polished
the clouds look like they're bouncing right in your face.

Dwayne and me had an argument about it.
He said it cost too much. I said I'd scrimp.
Sometimes it's hard to be a proper wife.
I don't like going against Dwayne.

You've got to give your kids advantages.
I never saw a swing till I started school.
Dwayne had it worse. Maybe that's what's wrong.

The rooms next door are rented, but we don't know who
or whether they'll have kids the right age.
Or whether we'll want them to. I'm nervous about it.
What if they smell? What if they talk funny?
There'll be hell to pay with Dwayne, I'll tell you.

And what if they're the kind to disappear,
to move away in the night, loading the car
with what all they can take, stealing something,
maybe taking the whole swing set?

What would I ever say to Jimmy?
Dwayne would cuss me first, then call the police.

I'm glad we have the set. I truly am.
This way, Jimmy can pick and choose his friends.

I know what Dwayne will do if who moves in
isn't right. Whoever it is, I tell you,
better not be single, pregnant and five kids,

and using food stamps. Or plop herself
and her cigarettes down every morning in my kitchen.
Or mess with that little tree.
I just hope they're clean.

A Southerner in Kansas Recalls Trees

Living without them, she takes solace
in hedges or in weeds.
Some nights,
alone in the house,
she lies face down on the wood floor.

JUST OFF THE HIGHWAY

It is an ugly spread.
Everything leans, even the house.
The grounds are bare, the butane tank and the shed
aloof in dirt.
Afternoons, a train sends sounds
that ripple under the grass.
Someone in the house opens a window part way and plays,
on what is still a piano,
"You Are My Lucky Star."

A FARMER DIES

He leaves ninety acres and a house.
In the kitchen,
a bowl of dusty pears.
In the orchard, leaves are turning to rust
as if it might not ever
rain again.
Someone will have to stay and sell the cows.

FEAR

A man and wife
sit at a delicatessen.
A young woman strolls in.
With her come sun and rain
and stars over a clear lake.
The man looks at the girl
in a way his wife has almost forgotten.

AIR MIDWEST LANDS ON ICE AT KANSAS CITY INTERNATIONAL

We taxi onto the apron
fast and slow and fast
as if the plane is looking for the dock.
Slowly I remember another evening.
Summer fishing with my grandfather,
caught by the dark, stragglers
looking for the right house and pier.
My grandfather finds the slot
and slips us in,
the outboard sputtering to silence
and smelling like a match just struck.
A light from my grandmother's kitchen
dozes on the water.

NEEDING NOISE

After the child died,
the mother and the father ran the accident
continually in their minds.
It repeated itself like an old teacher.
Sooner or later
the remaining children fell
from their parents' lives.

Days moved like stones.
The cocktail hour. The evening meal.

They watched television,
night after night,
disappointed.

SHE FEELS OUT OF PLACE IN BURL'S AUTO SERVICE

She gets out of her car.
A man, holding his Automotive Ready-Light,
slides under a lifted truck.
A man in coveralls strolls toward her.
On the radio, a country singer decides
about women and men.

THE YOUNG DRESSMAKER, BEST IN
EMERSON COUNTY

Everybody who knew anything about dressmaking
said it was a shame
a person didn't wear the garments Vera Hefley made
so you could see the wrong side.
They admired
the vanishing points of the darts,
the graceful easing of the set-in sleeves.

I thought
she should have been dancing.
A man should have had his hand
at the small of her back.
They should have been in a tango
back and forth
throughout that miserable house.

A Bottomlands Farmer's Widow Remarries and Speaks of the Killing

There's not much to tell different from anybody's
tale of woe. One summer we owned the Lincoln,
next we didn't. Too much sun, then it rained all March.
Mother blamed the Lincoln on Darrell—that was my husband.
She said he was drinking. Would you like a Scotch?

After the Lincoln went, things got bad.
More rotted crops, then Darrell and the trial,
then Mother died. Times when night comes down
smelling like a cottonmouth, I can see her
there at the trial, that satisfied look she got
when the lawyers held up the panty hose and bra
Darrell was supposed to be wearing the night he was killed.
A certain waitress named Nelda testified
he'd got drunk that night hustling three boys.

I got married again last Christmas. The farm was auctioned
right off the courthouse steps. My new husband, Jared,
he takes old Lincolns and fixes them up like new.
Those boys, they got thirty years apiece.

I barely think about it anymore.
A scale of one to ten, I'd put it six,
what with the farm and the baby and my oldest, Ginny,
which I don't know to this day
where she is.

DREAMING THE KIN

Climbing that dark hill again,
I see my grandfather in a field of corn.
I wave to him. He doesn't see me.
I move on to the barn
where dust motes hang like stars
in an unsteady heaven.

I enter my grandmother's kitchen.
Canning sausage, she doesn't look up.
My aunt sits folding clothes, her back to me.
Laughing, they speak of people I've never known.
Perhaps I've come to the wrong house,
though the table is set with the dishes I remember—
white, with red and yellow flowers chipping on the rims.

AFTER VIETNAM/STANDING AT A WINDOW AT GATE 2

A flight comes in.
The coffin, out of Baggage,
glistens like an ocarina.
So lightly she might be caressing a burn,
a woman touches the window.

MANY MANSIONS

Ernestine came Thursdays
to do my mother's wash.
She was black and smelled of starch,
her voice polite as the breeze
that tapped the kitchen curtains.
The child she brought with her one summer
sat on the back stoop and never spoke.

His eyes, storm dull and solemn,
come to mind as I think of my mother in her last days
when she seemed to see something so desolate
she could not turn away.

I guessed the boy to be four or five.
Ernestine didn't know.
He was her sister's boy,
sent down from Chicago.

AFTER A NEIGHBOR'S HOUSE WAS BROKEN INTO

She said it was like falling asleep in a rented room
and the landlord comes,
singing an aria from *Aida,*
snapping open the blinds like you'd snap green beans
and helping himself to chocolates on the table.

ADMISSION

On the outskirts of a carnival near Pueblo
a fox and a shrike amble by.
In a quarter-turn the fox becomes a man,
the shrike a woman.
He smiles through his rusty mustache.
Her polished nails curl inward
as she links her arm in his,
resting a hand on his sleeve.
They enter
the sizzling lights.

DRIVING A LOUISIANA HIGHWAY, PAST A TOWN WITH A RUINED DEPOT, SHE REMEMBERS THE NEGRO ALBINO IN HER HOMETOWN

His lips were too thick for the whites
and the blacks didn't like his freckles
and red hair.
Each summer Saturday,
sitting on my parents' porch,
I'd see the albino cutting the Brylie sisters' yard,
pushing the mower lazily back and forth
while one or the other sister watched.
     Thinking they knew just what caused some albinos,
     everybody in town named the white father,
     a former mayor who'd died of cancer
     and left his farm to the church.
The mowing finished,
the albino would wait on the back steps
until one of the sisters, fanning herself,
opened the screen door a notch
and handed him a dollar.

For years I haven't thought of the albino.
Now, driving past this town,
I see the years and towns. I see the one
I'll probably die a stranger in,
like him.

A PICTURE

In this picture
my mother younger than I am now
is in the kitchen,
singeing pin feathers over the gas range.
My brother is five and has not yet fallen
beneath the tractor.

IN RAY'S CAFE

A girl in a far booth
is breast-feeding a baby.
The man sitting across the table from me
stirs his coffee.
Where were you last night till 4 A.M., I say.
Someone starts the jukebox.
The girl shifts the baby to her shoulder
while she talks on the phone.
The baby wails.
The man sitting across from me signals the waitress,
careful not to break the noise between us.

WHAT PART OF TOWN WAS THAT IN?

A boy and a girl sit on a park bench.
Stick figures.
As I walk toward them, they draw themselves
fingernails and noses.
> *The gun as dull as stovepipe.*
> *They will take my earrings*
> *and my watch.*
Passing them, I glance behind me.
I see them on the park bench,
erasing their fingernails and noses,
stick figures again.
I walk on,
past brightening houses.

MY MOTHER'S DEAD DRESSES

They wake me from sleep.
Peach, magenta, red,
her young dresses
my father loved to touch.
They are 1940s dresses,
some with tiny zippers at the waist.
I wonder where in that lost house
my father has put them.

VAST

She took a snapshot of Kansas in June.
Endless sky blue as L.A. swimming pools,
endless grass green as Kentucky.
She framed it, hung it on the wall.
Turning from the room,
she didn't hear the avalanche,
sky and grass
spilling endlessly out of the frame.

Someone will find her
in due time.

HOW IT SOMETIMES HAPPENS TO A MAN THAT A NOBLE HEART AND PURPOSE COME TO DWELL WITHIN HIM

A man goes home to his wife,
thinking of a woman he has been with
that afternoon.
Kissing his wife and taking off his coat,
    he remembers how the woman
    unbuttoned her blouse.
After supper he sits with his drink on the darkening porch.
He would like to give to the woman
his love, his life, his father's
pocket watch.
He hears his wife
knitting in the dark.

SINGER AT THE FARMERS' MARKET

Walking onto the makeshift stage
she thinks how she can never
lay down all she knows,
the suicides of friends, two marriages failed,
a daughter gone morose and wrong.

Tonight, in this open arena, a breeze lifts her hair.
Her voice frays a little in the damp air
to bring the people back to the old loves,

a house, a street, a town.

DEPOT

Unchanged in thirty years,
they sometimes step onstage
beside that depot
where my husband and I first saw them
in a Georgia town we were driving through at dawn:
    A father and son, or so I've imagined them,
        the son in Army uniform extending his hand to the man
        who hesitates and turns away.
I saw a father's rejection of a son.
My husband saw an ongoing struggle
against despicable tears.
Thus they came to live inside our lives,
keeping their ordinary secrets to themselves.

A Story to Tell

Red's Tree Service was printed in an arc
across the dented pickup door.
She noted the men's tattoos.
She looked down at her blouse,
checking the buttons.

She pointed to the pin-oak a storm had uprooted.
The men walked around it. They argued.
They quoted a price.
It seemed to be within reason.

Still, standing there with them in the drive,
she told them Thanks but no.
Then she saw the girl, eighteen maybe,
sitting inside the truck, half smiling,
as if this is what you ought to expect
in a place where everybody has three-car garages
and ferns on their porch. Hadn't
she said?

Pulling the rusty pickup back into the street,
the driver grated through the gears.

The woman hesitated in front of the house.
Maybe she'd paint the trim a yellow.
Or a blue.

Later she invited the couple next door for drinks
on the glassed-in porch.
From somewhere down the street, the sounds of children.
A wasp in the room
shuffled its wings like paper.

She told them the story: The men. The tree.
She didn't mention
the girl.
The couple gave her a name to call—
somebody who would do a good job,
somebody who had been around for years.

SHE PONDERS THE DOCTOR'S DIAGNOSIS

The wind before a storm
flushes a paper sack out of a ditch.
The grasses in the ditch quiver.
She thinks of her mother so recently under ground,
in a frenzy of being changed.

EVERYTHING YOU WANTED

It sits beside a hill north of a town
named Miner's Grove or Franklin,
a farmhouse like any other in Kansas:
two-storied, white, bleak under four trees.
Behind it a windmill, a barn, a shed.
In the barn, the flaring smell of dung.
Room by room
sunlight blooms in the house,
polishes each table like a wife.
Here is everything
you wanted.

Someone enters stage left,
a husband maybe, or the eldest son
to hang himself in the cloudy breath of the milking shed.

ADDRESS

A policeman, sent to tell the husband,
goes by moonlight to the address in the woman's wallet
and rings the front bell.
He looks through the narrow window beside the door.
The husband comes, finally,
checking his watch.

A NICE TOWN

Driving north on Highway 17,
she takes the bypass around Eunice.
That's a nice town, she thinks,
the trees and the post office, the Baptist church,
the Tiptoe Lounge.
She stops and gets out, lifts the town like flagstone
and puts it on the seat beside her.

I DESCRIBE TO MY FURNITURE A HOUSE I MAY BUY

My sofa wants it,
wants to dig into the carpet
its pig legs.
The dining table can't wait to tap
its toenails into the vinyl.
Every night they set up a clamor.
Buy it! Buy it!

I remind them
they've been wrong before.

A Bottomlands Farmer's Wife Speaks after Attempting Suicide

I know it is a sin.
But Lord I was tired. The older kids scraping in
and out of the trailer,
the steaming diapers,
the promise of checks he'll send.
Here come the police, driving like hell to catch their sirens.
When they stop,
they'll slam the shiny doors of their cars
hard as they can.
I used to dread that sound. I liked it too.
Like my mother's voice shouting me to come in
or else.

THE ROAD

It is shorter, the trees lining it more sparse,
than when I went down it last.
The house at the end of it—
was it always that color?
And what happened to the glider
that used to sit on the porch?

A woman opens the screen door,
shutting it softly
the way I remember my grandmother doing.
The road lengthens. The trees lean toward each other
and touch.
The house is the right color;
in the glider on the porch
my uncle is rocking, reading *Forever Amber,*
refusing to tell me the story.

DRIVING ALONE

An hour now
and not another car.
Sunset takes the light, the sound.
She reaches for the radio,
already on.

FOR ALL THEY KNOW

A man became bored with his children.
They brought him family photographs;
they asked him to tell the stories.

He told them nothing,
dreaming his life
as if they had never been.

He might have ferried camels over the world's
great deserts. Been a duffer in Spokane.
Danced in Salzburg with Garbo.
For all they know.

A BEGINNING

The couple coming to view the doublewide
tell themselves it looks like a house.
You can't hardly tell where they put it together, she says,
taking the man's arm. Look at the shutters.
It'll need paint, he says, walking closer,
putting on and taking off his cap.

The young salesman crossing the gravel lot
curses the heat, needing a cigarette.
He points out the size of the living room,
that the previous owners didn't have pets.

The woman sees herself putting up curtains.
She'll need to paper the bath. She'll ask the man
to build a deck, after work, on Sundays.
They'll get a dog, plant zinnias in the back.

The salesman ushers them into a steamy office.
He jokes, taking some papers out of a desk,
and a fat maroon pen. The man says
they might be back tomorrow, that he and the woman
will have to talk. But he sees her face is brighter
than sometimes when they make love, brighter even

than when they were married. He sits down with the salesman,
shuffling through the papers, not reading them,
seeing their bedroom in his mother's house
where his wife is spreading a shirt to iron.

He is afraid in a way he has never been.

BUZZARDS NEAR OSAWATOMIE

Until one of them spread his wings
in front of the sun
like combs of translucent tortoise,
she didn't see the four of them,
black as the shed's black roof they perched upon.

When one floated down the side of the shed
to ease into shadows
where a door had been,
she wanted to go home,
marry the house and the children.

AT DARK

Night falls at the open air concert.
The stage is empty and dark.
Then the lone guitarist takes a step,
bringing with him the light.

In the front row,
bits of mirrors from a girl's dress
murmur like stories told from porches
as a mockingbird calls,
as green yards die into moonlight.

SEEING HER

A woman pilfering the dumpsters
in Monroe, Louisiana
sees dreams in the heat
that shimmers across the streets and bayous.
She knows what she needs:
A silky dress. Perfume.
Shoes with straps to tie at the ankle.
With these she might find
the man who, seeing her, can see
the columned house, the silver,
the deeply polished floors.

WAR BRIDE 1943

She's Betty Grable in platform shoes.
He's Dana Andrews.
She lights the candles and pours wine.
Everybody says
the war will be over soon.
The bride and her husband
drink to that.
From the radio, songs:
Tea for Two, Mairzy Doats,
and *When the Lights Go on Again.*
Closing the door behind them now,
they step out on the town.
When he ships out,
she'll go to stay with his mother
in Des Moines.

BASEBALL IN AMERICA

It's what some of us still count on,
always in the background
desultory and insistent
like trains, or mothers.

THE SUIT

Awake, asleep,
the woman dreams a suit to its perfection:
red silk,
crisp peplum,
lining pink as a conch.

Impostors come. More will.
But the woman and the suit
wait for each other.
It burns to sit upon her shoulders,
to button itself firmly about her ribs.

She longs to give herself to it.
Its red will be the red of parrots.
It will fit like an old despair.
It will bite its beholders' eyes.

I Drive into a Town for the First Time

Wind wraps around a town
wrapped around a courthouse square.
The town's only bank
sits beside the town's only tree.
The customers of the East Side Cafe look up,
look up again
as I walk in and take a seat.
The faces are vaguely familiar,
the old names swimming a slow crawl
to meet them.
A man touches his cap and comes toward me—
Fred Simpson, how long has it been—
his smile meant for another table.

How Life Sometimes Is Like Kansas

Think of yourself in a car
meeting an 18-wheeler
on a gray highway
under the bluest sky in America.
The ordinary clouds have all found their places.
You and the truck meet and pass
without a sound.
Think of fingers slammed in a car door,
of that moment
before the body is given notice.

BURYING MY FATHER

At the cemetery

the casket is taken out of the hearse
and placed carefully
before the disinterested chairs.

The preacher's words. The people.
Across the highway,
the reassuring hum

of a mowing machine.
I think of the other machine that will come
to put the coffin beside my mother's,

under the double stone.
Overhead
a knot of birds banks into the sun,

erasing itself.

LONG LIVES

In a small town
a man and a woman, evenings,
go out their separate garden gates
to take walks together,
to talk politics and roses and the way weeds can grow
on crocodiles' backs.
These are the ways they touch,
their voices falling and lifting
in the dark.

A Great Plains Farmer Beseeches the Lord for Rain

We've come a long way from you, Lord,
a fact most of us acknowledge.
Sinners, all, but we do suffer.
The few trees left are shriven.
The ground divides and shifts,
a peril to dogs and children
and cattle worse off than Job's.
Everywhere about us, commandments break.

Elmer Brantlee's wheat dried up;
rumor has it the bank will foreclose.
I warrant it doesn't matter much
in the scheme of things. The radio
says rain. But who can believe?

I owe the bank more than I'll let on.
The wife, she's taken to smiling less:
there's no money now for those things she craves.

And there is this minor thing
a rain might ease:
she sleeps—because of the heat, she claims—
as far from me in bed as ever she can.

So, Lord, . . . if I am just, and if you please.

JO MCDOUGALL is the author of three books of poetry, including *Towns Facing Railroads* (University of Arkansas Press, 1991). A native of DeWitt, Arkansas, she teaches English and creative writing at Pittsburg State University in Pittsburg, Kansas.